SO-FAI-771

I WANT TO KNOW ABOUT
THE UNITED STATES SENATE

I WANT TO KNOW ABOUT

THE UNITED STATES SENATE

Senator Charles Percy

Conceived and Produced
by Whitehall, Hadlyme & Smith, Inc.

DOUBLEDAY & COMPANY, INC.
GARDEN CITY, NEW YORK

Library of Congress Cataloging in Publication Data

Percy, Charles H 1919–
    I want to know about the United States Senate.

        1. United States. Senate—Juvenile literature.
I. Whitehall, Hadlyme & Smith.   II. Title.
III. Title: The United States Senate.
JK1276.P47   328.73′07′1
ISBN 0-385-09679-8 Trade
        0-385-00192-4 Prebound
Library of Congress Catalog Card Number 76–158
Copyright © 1976 by Whitehall, Hadlyme & Smith, Inc.

CONTENTS

BEING A SENATOR 1

GETTING INTO POLITICS 21

WHAT GOES ON 33

SOME CONCERNS 55

SOME FOND MEMORIES 67

IN THE FUTURE 73

INDEX 81

I WANT TO KNOW ABOUT
THE UNITED STATES SENATE

It's important to stay on top of the news.

BEING
A SENATOR

My job is never boring. In fact, it's the most exciting possible line of work—for me, at least. I'm involved in lawmaking. I'm involved in science. I'm involved in education. I'm involved in foreign relations.

The days are long, but filled with activity. My workday generally begins at about 6:30 A.M. I read the newspapers that are delivered to my door, along with a copy of *The Congressional Record*, which is also delivered. It contains the entire proceedings of the House and the Senate from the day before—what was said and done by whom.

Twice a week I try to play tennis at 7:00 in the morning. That's usually the only time of day that I can play, because I can hardly ever leave the office before 7:00 in the evening. And even then, on most days, I still have work to do. On the days when I'm not playing tennis in the morning, I try to catch the "Today" program on television, but I often must watch it while I shave. Then I try to leave the house by 8:15 in order to get to the office by 8:30 or so.

What would a senator do without a phone?

On most days, if I get to the office by then, I have about an hour to spend answering mail and phone calls and reviewing legislative activities. Sometimes I meet with one or two staff members to discuss specific problems that will come up during the day.

The Senate has many committee meetings. Here I am with Senator Abraham Ribicoff of Connecticut during a meeting of the Permanent Investigations Subcommittee of the Senate.

Once a week there is a staff meeting at 8:30 A.M. It lasts for about a half hour, and every member of my Washington staff is there. Each department head

3

reports on what his or her department did during the previous week. The department heads also tell of their plans for the week to come.

At 10:00 in the morning, the Senate's committee meetings begin. I am now serving on nineteen committees and subcommittees in the Senate. Obviously some of these meetings will overlap, so I have to make decisions about which ones I will attend on a given day. Sometimes I testify before these committees, but most often I am listening to the testimony of others or questioning witnesses.

These committee meetings can last past noon, but, generally speaking, the Senate convenes at noon. Many times it starts earlier, but noon is the latest. By the way, if a senator wants to give a short speech on the floor of the Senate, the time to do it is during what we call our "morning hour," after the formal opening of the session. This time is reserved for any senator who wishes to make a speech on any subject.

When the legislative program begins on the Senate floor, we try to be there if something that we are interested in is being discussed. We want to express our own views on the matter or listen to the views of others. We also want to be present when there is going to be a vote on a legislative matter.

Somehow or other we have to try to squeeze in lunch. Usually these are working lunches. Often these working lunches are held in my office over box lunches that have been sent in. Mealtime is a great time to exchange ideas.

In the afternoon, while the legislative session is still going on, there can be many other interruptions. If people want to see me during the day, they generally have to come up to the Senate reception room, because on the Senate floor only senators, pages, and others who work there are allowed. The visitors send a note in with a page asking to see me. Then, unless I happen to be speaking or about to speak, I will come out to see them.

The first time that I was in this situation, I was not a senator. I was a businessman. I had sent in a note to the late Senator Robert Taft of Ohio asking if he would see me. I waited right there in the reception room until he came off the floor and we could discuss our business.

His meeting me like that so impressed me that I still try to see everybody who wants to see me. Sometimes these people are interested in a particular piece of information about some legislation. Sometimes they are just visitors from Illinois who want to meet their senator.

When the legislative session is over, usually about 5:30 or 6:00 in the evening, there is still work to do. When I get back to the office, there are many telephone calls to make. Then I have to sign the letters that have been typed for me and dictate new ones. Usually there are staff members still around who must talk with me.

If I'm lucky, I can make it home for dinner by about 8:00. But I have to carry a big briefcase full of work home with me.

Often Mrs. Percy and I go out in the evening. I am on the Foreign Relations Committee of the Senate, so we are often invited to dinners or receptions at the various embassies. This keeps us up on what is going on in other parts of the world and lets Mrs. Percy participate.

Let me give you an example. I recently went to a dinner at the Indian Embassy. There were dignitaries

Sometimes I have a lot of fun with my visitors. Once the entire band from Harrisburg, Illinois, dropped in to see me. You can probably tell that I don't know much about playing the clarinet.

It's toward the end of a long day, and I still have a telephone growing out of my ear.

When I get back home to Illinois, I like to meet with political leaders . . .

from all over the world there. In addition, there was the Chief Justice of the United States Supreme Court and many members of the executive and legislative branches of the government. You can learn a lot at these parties. And the nice thing about them is that they usually begin at 8:00 and end promptly at 11:00.

Then come the weekends. It used to be, when I was in private business, that when Friday night came, I was ready to relax for two days. Not now. Here is a typical example. On a Friday night I flew to Kentucky to make a speech. Weekends are the best time for

. . . and talk to voters. This gentleman is quite unusual. He lives in Springfield and is one hundred and one years old.

making speeches away from Washington, since you are not interfering with your working week. This one was a speech to help a senator who was up for re-election. Saturday I flew to Chicago to talk with constituents. I returned to Washington late on Sunday. Add to this my guess that, on the average, we spend at least two weekends in Illinois every month. So we can't relax much on weekends.

You might wonder about those long congressional recesses that you have heard about. Most of these are not really vacations. I must go all over the state of

Travel abroad can be very important. Some things have to be seen to be believed—for example, the Berlin Wall. (COURTESY OF ELISABETH PERCY)

And I also like to talk with people who are not old enough to vote. Here I am with a very special little boy.

Illinois talking with people to find out what their problems are and how I can help them. I must also spend time at my Chicago and Springfield offices.

I must also make official trips abroad. One time, on a trip to the Middle East, I visited thirteen countries—eleven Arab countries, Iran, and Israel—all in twenty-three days.

There is a little time to do other things. I serve as a trustee of the University of Chicago and am also on the board of the Kennedy Center for the Performing Arts. I was once chairman of the Fund for Adult Education of the Ford Foundation. This is the group that set up the program for public television. I have a deep interest in the work of foundations and educational institutions.

That's the working life of a senator. In addition to legislative activities, there are hundreds of thousands of letters to be written each year. There are tens of thousands of phone calls to be answered. There are countless numbers of visitors to be seen.

You have probably guessed that I cannot do all of that by myself. I have a great staff of between forty and fifty members. Some of them are full-time workers and some of them are unpaid volunteers. Most of the staff members are located in Washington, but I also have small staffs in Springfield, the capital of Illinois, and Chicago, the largest city in the state.

By now I must have given the impression that the life of a senator consists of nothing but work, work, work. That's not exactly true. Once in a while there are literally fun and games in Washington.

For example, like many senators, I maintain a baseball team. That is, the staff and I sometimes play baseball with the staff of another senator. I like to fancy myself as a second baseman, but I will never forget the time that I dropped a fly ball that was hit by Senator Adlai Stevenson III. That was the game for the championship of the state of Illinois, Capitol Branch. Fortunately, we won despite my error.

We have a lot of fun in these games, as you can tell by reading this hot news flash:

LITTLE MIRACLE ON 37TH STREET

Washington, June 18. Trailing by eleven—that's right, eleven—runs before they came to bat for the first time, the Percy Kewshuns [How is that for a terrible pun?] kept their famous cool Tuesday night and roared back to defeat the Javits Jets, 23–18.

The Percy team seemed to have no more chance than a Republican candidate in the first ward after the Jets sent eleven runners scampering home in the top of the first inning against the defense described by one seasoned observer as "modest, at best."

But the Kewshuns, appearing visibly relaxed under the burden, chipped away at the deficit as though it were the national debt. They scored two in the first, eight in the second, and four more in the third to take the lead. Another eight-run burst in the fourth inning wrapped up the Kewshuns' fourth victory in five softball starts this season on the home field on 37th and Quebec Avenue.

Ed Hughes and Greg Ward led the Percy uphill climb with two homers apiece. Alison Kothe and winning pitcher Rita Green enjoyed a banner evening at bat, each reaching the base four times.

Coach Donna Maddox, rotating players with the aplomb of a young Casey Stengel, worked all twenty Percy staffers present into the lineup.

"This was just a warmup," Maddox warned later. "The true test of our grit will come against Stevenson on Monday, July fourteenth."

Sometimes we have nonworking parties, and they can be fun. I remember seeing Jack Kennedy in a cowboy outfit at a party once. Another time I was giving a party during the Johnson Administration and invited Art Buchwald, the newspaper columnist. He wrote back to tell me that he would be there unless President Johnson called him to the White House to ask what he should do next in Vietnam.

Every Christmas I have a party for my staff at my home. They repay me for this party by putting on funny skits about our office life. Unfortunately, very few of these skits are flattering to me. But we all have a good time.

As I mentioned before, I am also interested in sports. In college, I wrestled and was on the water polo team. Now I often play tennis with Senator Lowell Weicker of Connecticut or Senator Dewey Bartlett of

Oklahoma. I guess I'm better as a doubles player than a singles player, but one thing I'm very proud of is that I have played Democratic Governor Daniel Walker of Illinois twice—once in Washington and once in Illinois—and eked out a victory both times.

I try to swim whenever I can. We have a very small pool in the Senate, but it gives us a chance to take a break once or twice a week to get in a little exercise.

My favorite sport is skiing. When I take a vacation, it usually takes me about three days to unwind. However, when I go skiing, I am completely relaxed after one trip down the slopes.

There is something exciting about going forty miles an hour down a snowy hill on a couple of boards. It almost makes me forget about the Senate for a while. This doesn't happen when you are playing golf. You hit your shot and then think about your problems while you are walking up to where the ball landed.

But there's something about skiing. Maybe it's because there is no phone on the ski trail. Maybe it is the wonderful companionship before, during, and after a day in the outdoors. It helps me unwind.

Whenever I get a chance, I visit with my children in West Virginia, Seattle, and California. On the trips to West Virginia, some of my happiest times are spent with my three grandchildren. Grandchildren are great. You have all the fun of being with little ones, and yet you are not responsible for their upbringing.

I like to make up stories for them, too. Usually these stories are about a couple of mice that I have invented. But the grandchildren insist on helping me

*A Jimmy Connors I'm not. But at least I've learned to get
my racket back while waiting for the ball.* (GUY DELORT
PHOTO FROM WOMEN'S WEAR DAILY)

My favorite sport.

Maybe I've always liked children. Here I am at the age of five hugging my baby sister. My brother seems to be more interested in the cameraman. (COURTESY OF ELISABETH PERCY)

with the stories. Before I start, they will tell me that they want a new story and then they list the things that they want in it. They may want a witch, a thunderstorm, an airplane, a magic castle, and a cave. Then, when the story is over, they may point out that I have forgotten to put in the magic castle. This makes the story even longer, of course, but it's fun.

So that's what I do at work and at play. If I am asked whether or not I like being a senator, I answer, "I love it." Today, I don't think that I would trade being an elected official for the world.

The young naval officer in 1943. (COURTESY OF ELISABETH PERCY)

GETTING
INTO
POLITICS

THE WHOLE THING BEGAN when I came back
from World War II in 1946. I had served for two years
as the commanding officer of the Advance Base Aviation
Training Units in the 13th, 14th, and 15th Naval Districts. For my third year in service, I was attached to the
Naval Air Corps as a gunnery officer.

So here I was, back home again, working as a
businessman in Chicago for the Bell & Howell Company.
At that time, Bell & Howell was specializing in the manufacture of cameras, although they later went into other
areas as well.

I had been graduated from the University of
Chicago and had also taken some law classes at night
school. So I was becoming more and more interested in
law and more and more convinced that lawmaking was
an extremely important field. I guess I was beginning to
feel that politics was too important to leave to the politicians.

Long before, I had decided that I was a Republican. Maybe the only reason for this was that my mother and father were Republicans. If they had been Democrats, I might have been a Democrat. This line of reasoning doesn't always hold true, of course. My son-in-law, Jay Rockefeller, is a Democrat, and you would have to look a long time to find anything but Republicans in that family—except for Jay.

So, in 1946, with two friends, Art Nielsen, now the chairman of A. C. Nielsen Company, and Bud Rothemal, I formed a group called Veterans for the Republican Party. And we tried to get all other returning veterans to work in the Republican party.

Our first job was to work for a Republican who was running for Congress in that election year. After the campaign, I became an assistant precinct captain in my home community north of Chicago.

Within the next few years I became president of Bell & Howell. And I was the Illinois State Finance Chairman of the Republican National Committee. There were also times when I was asked to take on different jobs for the Republican party.

One of these jobs was to serve on a study group called the Rockefeller Brothers Studies Project, which examined the whole area of American and world problems and tried to determine what the role of our country would be in the future. Out of this came a report that was called "Prospects for America."

Then came my personal turning point. The election year of 1958 had not been a good one for the Republican party, and we were concerned about what we could do to rebuild our party. But first I decided that I needed a post-election vacation.

With my son-in-law, Jay Rockefeller. Obviously Republicans and Democrats can get along together.

I was skiing in Sun Valley, Idaho, over Christmas of that year when I received a telegram from President Eisenhower. He asked me to attend a meeting at the White House early in 1959.

Truthfully, I didn't want to miss any days on the slope, so I called Washington to find out whether the meeting was important or not. I really didn't know whether the request had come from the President or had been thought up by someone on the staff.

The presidential assistant that I talked to had not heard of the telegram, so he promised to check on it. As it turned out, the President had thought up the idea for the meeting himself, had drafted the telegram himself, and really wanted me to come.

Our group of Republican leaders met with President Eisenhower and reviewed the disastrous 1958 Republican political results. When he asked for suggestions, I proposed that we set up a Commission on National Goals. The commission would be headed by a prominent person, and the members would be selected from both Republican and Democratic parties. Once the goals were outlined, the Republican party could establish a committee that would show how Republicans thought they might achieve those goals. I also hoped that the Democrats would do the same.

I thought that this would be good for the country. I thought that the committees could come up with an answer to the question "Where should we be as a nation by 1976—our bicentennial?" The President was also enthusiastic and invited me back to the White House the next day.

It turned out that he was working on his State of the Union message and wanted to add a request to set up the Commission on National Goals to his speech. We spent the day working on this part of the speech. After we had finished he invited me back to the White House residence section for a friendly chat.

I'll never forget that talk. I found out about the President's humility and learned of his loyalty.

I think his humility was never so apparent to me as it was during our private discussion. He was talking about his brother Milton Eisenhower, who, among other things, was president of Johns Hopkins University. The president put his arm around my shoulder and said, "Milton is the brightest of the Eisenhower brothers. He was the one who really should have been President, not me."

He also made me an offer, and over the years I learned of his loyalty. When he said he would support a person, he meant it. This time he told me that he hoped that I would run for public office myself one day, and that he would support me for such office "be it the highest in the land."

The State of the Union message was given. It included a request for the commission. President Eisenhower asked me to be the head of the commission, but I had to refuse. I was too much a Republican to head a nonpartisan group such as this. I gladly accepted his invitation to be the chairman of the Republican Committee on Program and Progress, though. This was the group that published a report on what we thought our party ought to do to achieve the goals of the commission.

After nine months of work, our report, "Decisions for a Better America," was published. I have always thought it was my work on this committee that caused me to be named chairman of the 1960 Platform Com-

President Eisenhower did support me. That's a Percy button he's wearing on his lapel.

mittee of the Republican National Convention. And that job at the convention led to my full-time entry into politics.

My family and I had a little problem when I was thinking about running for office. I had been president and chairman of the board of a large company. But I had spent twenty-five years at Bell & Howell

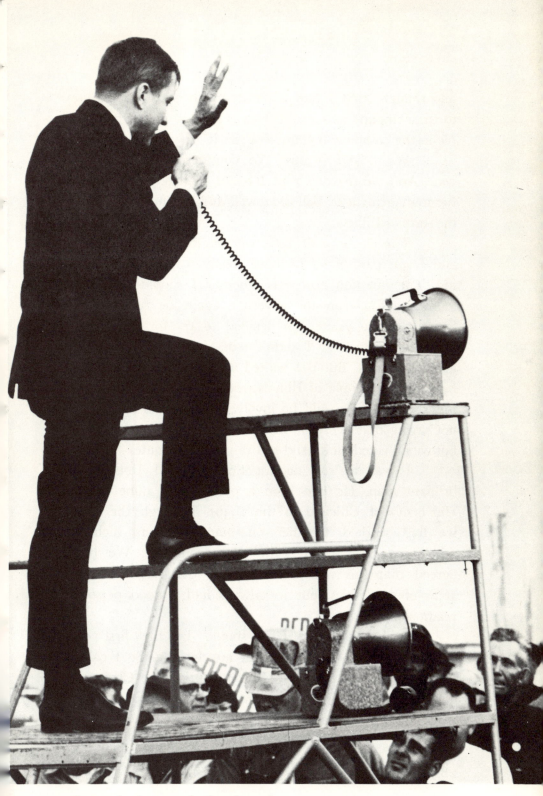

Campaigning can be hard work.

and thought that I had made as much of a contribution to the company as I could. It was time to give other people in the company a chance to run it.

We talked it out. We considered the pros and cons. And we decided that I ought to take a leave from the management of Bell & Howell and run for governor of the state of Illinois.

The elections of 1964 were a Republican disaster, and I was part of it. So it was back to the family meeting. The question now was whether I should wait four more years to run for governor again or run for the Senate in two years. We decided to try for the Senate and keep going. If I didn't win, I could still try for governor again. But if I waited and did nothing, perhaps by 1968 the people of Illinois would have forgotten about me, or maybe I would be involved in business again. I'm not saying that everyone in the family had an equal vote, but we all voted on it. And so I ran for the Senate.

I was to run against Senator Paul Douglas—a brilliant man. He had been a professor of mine at the University of Chicago in the 1930s. Through the years we had worked together on many projects such as developing freer trade with other countries. We both agreed that this was necessary. We disagreed on some areas of economics, but we always had a good personal relationship.

I thought that Paul should be the first one outside my family to hear about my decision. So I called him at his vacation spot in Mexico during the Christmas holidays of 1965. I will always remember his response.

"I knew that someday you would have to run

During the campaign. The late Senator Everett Dirksen of Illinois is the man in the middle.

against me. I thought that you were going to do it in 1960. In fact, I asked if you were going to do it, and was relieved that you were not, as you were the only Republican who could have defeated me at the time. It is in the nature of the system that the best man in each party should run. I think that we can have a campaign based upon issues, not personalities."

I won. And after I had defeated Senator Douglas, I had to say to him that truthfully I felt bad that he had been defeated, but I would have felt worse if he had defeated me. It was hard, though, to speak so lightly

Nothing pleases me more than to have students become interested in politics.

to a man for whom I had such a high personal regard and who demonstrated his great intelligence, character, and devotion in so many ways through the years.

In 1972 I was re-elected for a second six-year term. And now that I have had the experience of winning twice, I know what a good feeling it can be. Especially since so many people have worked so hard to help get me elected. Let me give an example.

One of the happiest moments of my life—being sworn in as a member of the Senate. Here I am being given the oath of office by the then-Vice-president, Hubert Humphrey. At the left is Senator Mike Mansfield of Montana, and at the right is the late senior senator from Illinois, Everett M. Dirksen.

During my first try, the campaign for governor, I got a lot of help from high school students. The students in my old high school were so pleased that an old graduate was running for state office that they really got behind me.

Some of them organized a car wash every Saturday morning. They would wash cars for a dollar, and every dollar was donated to my campaign. I had a terrible time convincing them that they ought to deduct the cost of soap, water, and polishing cloths. They helped run my campaign office from five in the afternoon until ten at night. They ran the switchboard and the mimeograph machine and did many other things. High school students were a very important part of that campaign.

Some of them cried the night I lost. In some ways, they felt worse about it than I did. By the time I ran for the Senate, many of them were college students who were going to school in Illinois and they worked to help me again. You can bet they felt better after that campaign. Many are now active in politics.

I keep thinking of the young people who have helped me throughout my political career. I always hope that I have lived up to their expectations. They have done so much for me.

My second term in the Senate expires in 1978, and who knows what will happen then. Nothing is assured in politics. There are no guarantees and there is a lot of unemployment among politicians.

WHAT
GOES ON

IN ORDER TO UNDERSTAND where the Senate fits into our system of government, we have to look back to our country's beginning. Our Founding Fathers decided to form a government that included the idea of separation of powers. In order to do this, they set up three coequal branches of this government.

One of these three branches is the judicial branch. It includes the Supreme Court and all of the lesser federal courts.

Another of the branches is the executive branch. This includes the President and Vice-president. These are the only two offices in the country that are customarily elected by all of the people in the country—all of the people who can vote, of course. This branch, in addition, includes all of the men and women that the President appoints. So the executive branch also includes the members of the Cabinet, the departments they head, the ambassadors, the Joint Chiefs of Staff, and many, many other people.

The third branch is the legislative branch. These are the people who enact laws. This branch consists of the House of Representatives and the Senate. At the present time there are four hundred thirty-five members of the House, and they are called representatives or congressmen and congresswomen. The number of representatives per state varies according to the population of the state. For example, Alaska has only one representative, whereas my state, Illinois, has twenty-four. Every state is entitled to at least one person in the House, but the typical congressman or woman represents almost five hundred thousand people. These people make up his or her congressional district. Sometimes there are enough people in a single city, such as New York City or Chicago or Los Angeles, to make up several districts. The members of the House represent only the people in their own district, and the people in each district elect their own representative.

Representatives are elected for a two-year term, but the members of the United States Senate are elected for six years at a time. That is one of the longest terms of any elective office in the world. One of the few longer ones in a democracy is in France. Their President has a seven-year term.

The Senate is not set up in the same way as the House. The population of our states has nothing to do with how many senators are elected per state. Each of the fifty states has two senators, who are elected by all the voters in the entire state. So Alaska, with the smallest population of any state in the Union, has as many senators as the most populous state, California. Each of the states has, therefore, a "senior senator," who has served consecutively for the longest time, and a "junior senator."

A meeting in my Springfield office with Governor Dan Walker of Illinois (center) and Senator Adlai E. Stevenson III.

For example, I am the senior senator from Illinois, and Adlai E. Stevenson III is the junior senator. An interesting thing can happen here. As I mentioned, it is the length of consecutive service in the Senate that determines whether a senator is senior or junior. After years of being the senior senator from Arizona, Barry Goldwater resigned to run for President. When he was defeated, he decided to try to get his old Senate seat back again. He won, but in the meantime, Paul Fannin had already been elected as a senator from Arizona. Although Goldwater had served many more years than Fannin, he once again became the junior senator from Arizona because his length of service had been broken.

Some states have two Republican senators; others have two Democratic senators. The state of Illinois has one of each. The Senate is a really diverse group of one hundred people.

About the only thing that all senators share is that every one of them is over thirty years of age. That is the minimum age that a senator must be before taking office. There are people in the Senate whose families came from English, French, Lebanese, German, and African stock, and many more. There are Catholics, Protestants, and Jews in the Senate.

Most senators, probably seventy of the one hundred, have law degrees. It seems that when people study law, they often become interested in government, too. After all, laws are made by the government.

However, in the Senate, business, journalism, farming, and many other professions are also represented. I used to think it was odd that there were two or three farmers in the Senate. But then I thought of some of the other farmers who were so important in getting this country started—George Washington, Thomas Jefferson, and James Madison, for example.

One of our most distinguished former senators, Margaret Chase Smith, was neither a lawyer, a businesswoman, nor a farmer. She was, first and foremost, a concerned woman who was deeply interested in politics.

Many people wonder, considering the wide range

of interests and backgrounds in the Senate, who is in charge. Even the majority leader and the minority leader sometimes ask this question.

Officially, the Vice-president of the United States is the president of the Senate. But he would probably be the last person in the world to say that he is really in charge of the Senate. It is his job to preside over the Senate, which is the only duty given to the Vice-president by the Constitution. But he is not even permitted to vote on a bill unless there is a tie vote on the floor and his vote is necessary to break the tie. And that rarely happens.

He is also not allowed to speak on the floor of the Senate. There is an old story about something that happened to Martin Van Buren while he was Vice-president. Senator John C. Calhoun, his archrival, was on the floor, debating. Van Buren got interested in the debate, and, from the presiding officer's chair, started to enter into the discussion.

He got out about ten words before Senator Calhoun looked at him and roared, "By what right does the presiding officer, the president of the Senate, dare speak in the Senate on a substantive issue?"

Of course he had no right. And that is the last time, as far as I know, that any President of the Senate has dared try to enter into debate without prior consent of the Senate.

When the Vice-president is not in the Senate, his place will be taken by a senator. We take turns. But if a senator is acting as the presiding officer and gets interested in a debate, he cannot join in either.

There have been times when I was taking my turn as the presiding officer and I got so interested that I felt I had to say something. But I couldn't unless I

President Ford signs a bill while members of Congress look on.

beckoned to one of my fellow senators and asked him or her to come up and take my place. I then went down on the floor and became part of the discussion.

Unlike the Vice-president, when a senator is in the chair, he or she can vote when his or her name is called during a roll call.

So we get back to the question of who runs the Senate. There is a senator who is the leader of the majority party and one who is the leader of the minority party. They are assisted by the assistant leaders, called Republican and Democratic whips, who take care of party discipline, such as it is, and floor traffic. But nobody really runs the Senate because each senator is responsible, not to the leaders of the Senate, but to the people of his or her home state.

No one can tell a senator how to vote. No one can even force a senator to vote at all. Even the President can't give orders to a senator. Each of the Presidents who has been in the White House while I have been in the Senate—Johnson, Nixon, and Ford— has tried many times to get me to vote the way he wanted me to vote. But I refused as often as not.

In spite of the fact that there is really no Senate boss, we do manage to perform our most important duty—doing our part in making laws. Let's go over the process in which a bill becomes a law. And I would like to select a hot issue as an example—gun control.

Think for a minute. Do you think that handguns, the cheap so-called Saturday night specials, ought to be allowed to be sold on the streets of a city or anywhere else? Over a million of these weapons are sold every year in the United States at a price of between twenty and thirty dollars.

Every citizen has the right to suggest legislation.

These are little guns that fit into your pocket or purse and can be easily hidden. Even though almost everyone is against these guns, we do not have a national law that prevents their manufacture, distribution, or sale. These guns are not used for hunting, sports, or target practice. Policemen do not carry them. They are used only to injure or kill people illegally.

Suppose that you, as a citizen, decide that we ought to have a law prohibiting Saturday night specials. What would you do about it? First, you could write a letter to your senator or congressman.

Also suppose that you lived in Illinois. You might write to me and say that you think we ought to have a law prohibiting these guns. What happens next?

I read the letter and talk it over with my staff. I tell them that I think it is a good idea to have this law. But first it must be researched. We must find out about all the existing laws on handguns. Members of the staff go to the Legislative Reference Bureau in the Library of Congress to check out the laws. If there are weaknesses or loopholes in existing laws, as there are in this case, we will write a bill to take care of the problem.

I then introduce the bill into the Senate. It is printed up overnight. By this time, I may have found other senators who will want to join me in sponsoring this bill.

Next, the bill is sent to a committee for consideration. The parliamentarian of the Senate is the person who has the responsibility of choosing which of the many committees should study the bill. But the chances are that this bill will go to the Senate Judiciary Committee, and probably then to one of its subcommittees.

The committee may call public hearings. At this time, interested people, including you or me, can testify on the bill—pro or con.

Now who would testify against this bill? Possibly the manufacturers and distributors of these guns. Perhaps the gun dealers themselves would appear. Of course I, the other sponsors of the bill, and other concerned citizens would be testifying for it.

After the hearings, the subcommittee does what is called "marking up the bill." The members of the sub-

Part of the job of being a senator is to testify for or against a proposed piece of legislation.

committee can amend it or they can completely change it. Then they vote on it. They can vote not to consider it. They can vote to postpone a decision. They can vote to return it to the full committee. This meeting is open to the public.

Then there is another markup session in the full committee and possibly another hearing—this time also in public. The arguments are listened to and the committee votes. They can vote not to consider the bill. They can vote to postpone their decision. Or they can vote to send it to the floor of the Senate.

Suppose that they vote to send it to the Senate. It is then put on the calendar by picking a date when it will be debated. The date picked must be at least three days away to give the senators time to study the bill and decide whether to support it or not. If there are no hitches, it will be approved and passed by the Senate. But is it a law yet?

No. It must be sent to the House of Representatives. A messenger literally walks it over and stands in the back of the House. He calls for the attention of the Speaker of the House and announces that he bears "a message from the Senate."

Now the House goes through the same procedure that the Senate did. It refers the bill to a subcommittee; it is sent to the full committee; the hearings are held; the bill is presented to the House; and a vote is cast.

If the House passes a bill not quite identical to the Senate bill, a House-Senate conference is set up. The bill may be changed to iron out the differences of opinion between the House and the Senate. Then both the House and Senate vote on the bill again.

Once both the House and Senate approve the bill,

A bill must be debated.

it is sent to the President for his signature. But it is not a law until the President signs it.

If the President vetoes the bill—that is, if he turns it down—it is sent back to Congress. If the House and the Senate can come up with enough votes approving the bill again—two thirds of the members of each group—the veto has been overridden and the bill becomes a law. But something else can happen.

Perhaps a gun manufacturer feels that the law is unfair. He can take his case to court. He can go to the district federal court to challenge the constitutionality of the law. If he fails there, he can take his case to the appellate court. If he fails again, the Supreme Court may decide to hear his case. If one of these three courts decides that the law is unconstitutional, it can declare the law null and void. That means that it can no longer be enforced.

Congress can then take the law back to study the decision of the court. The House and the Senate may decide that they can change the law in such a way as to make it constitutional, and the whole process starts all over again. But this decision is rare.

This is a long-drawn-out process, and it is filled with many disagreements. Congressmen and senators have just as many disagreements as any other group of people. The citizens of our country are diverse, and Congress is no less diverse. We have many different viewpoints and ideas.

The gun law is an example of this. It is strongly supported in the cities. Chicago, as an example, has had more than eight hundred murders in a single year, many of them with the Saturday night special as the weapon. But the gun control law may not be supported in rural areas. Farmers often have guns at home and may feel that if we had gun control someone would take their weapons away from them.

This does not mean that rural people tend to support murder. They just have different ideas about gun control. City people might say that if there were no guns, crime would decrease. Country people might say that criminals will always be able to get guns, and this law would take away the protection of innocent people. It is difficult to say who is right and who is wrong.

But, for the most part, I think we have common goals. We want a secure, strong nation. We want a nation that lives up to the promise of equal opportunity for everyone. The problem is that there is a difference of opinion on how our programs should be carried out. We can agree on goals, but rural people do not always agree with urban people, or Northerners with Southerners, or Republicans with Democrats, or even Republicans with Republicans and Democrats with Democrats, on how we should achieve these goals.

Every time I talk about how a bill becomes a law, someone asks why it is such a slow process. The reason is that the process is designed to be slow. We have to think things through, take care, and debate the subject thoroughly. Many road blocks are purposely placed in the way of quick, swift decisions. Rapid decisions may look good at first glance, but on examination, they may not be the best decisions at all. These road blocks are also designed to prevent a person with evil intentions, no matter what position of power he or she may be in, from forcing his or her will on the nation.

The red tape can be cut when necessary, of course. There are times of emergency when we have to act quickly. For instance, people who have been hit by floods or tornadoes need help in a hurry. We can get a bill through very swiftly to provide relief funds. I have seen legislation go through both the House and the Senate and sent to the President in one day. Yet some bills take years to pass.

When I mention quick legislation, someone always brings up the matter of declaring war. War is declared suddenly. But in the recent past, our way of declaring war seems to have changed. It is a very profound problem because it goes to the heart of the Constitution and the separation of powers between the Congress and the President.

The Constitution says clearly, very clearly, that only Congress has the power to declare war. And if you were to go over all of the proceedings of our Constitutional Convention, you would see that this was what Madison and Jefferson and Hamilton and Adams intended.

Throughout our history, until just after World War II, we did not go to war until Congress had officially given the President permission to declare war. But since World War II, we have been at war with North Korea, North Vietnam, and portions of Laos and Cambodia without ever formally declaring war.

Along with several other senators, I felt that something was wrong with this. Because the President is also Commander in Chief of the Armed Forces, some of them have felt that they can take us to war without consulting Congress.

Feeling that there must be a legal flaw somewhere, Senator Javits of New York, with my support and the support of Senator John Stennis of Mississippi, introduced a resolution. The resolution called for a limitation in the war-making powers of the President.

It permits him to react to a sudden enemy attack, of course. Or he can send in troops for sixty days. But it is illegal for him to wage war for longer than that unless he has the approval of Congress.

This is all pretty grim, so let me mention one of the more pleasant duties that I have—appointing Senate pages.

Pages are the young people in the Senate chambers who have the task of running errands for the senators, delivering papers to their desks, and doing many other jobs. There are Republican pages to aid the Republican senators, and Democratic pages to aid the Democratic senators.

These young people are usually fifteen or sixteen years old. They must have good school records, be well rounded with a good personality, and be able to get along with others. They apply for the job, and there is a committee of senators to screen the applications. This committee recommends three applicants for each opening, and the final selection from the three is made by a senator appointed for that purpose. Right now there are six Republican pages.

When I first arrived in the Senate, I was, of course, the junior senator from Illinois. The senior senator from Illinois was the late Everett Dirksen, who was the minority leader at the time. He asked me if I would like the privilege of appointing Republican pages. He mentioned that he knew that I liked young people and that this would be a wonderful opportunity to appoint a page from the state of Illinois. Naturally, I said yes.

As I said, pages must be outstanding young people. But at that time, pages had to be outstanding young men. There were no female pages. We changed all that, and here is how we did it.

After my first few years of picking boy pages, I thought, "Why not appoint girl pages?" I talked with Senator Javits about it. He also wondered why we couldn't have female pages. Since Senator Javits is another senator who has the power of selecting pages, we both nominated girls.

There was an uproar in the Senate. Many members didn't know what to do about our proposal. They didn't want girls to be in the page school. They didn't want them on the floor of the Senate. They didn't want to pay them. When I asked why, I was told that it was a tradition in the Senate to have only male pages.

Again I asked why. But this time I demanded an explanation, in writing, of the real reasons that girls could not be pages. The first reason given was that girls in skirts would look unladylike when sitting on the steps of the floor of the Senate. I said that they could wear slacks.

Then they said that there was crime on the streets of Washington and the page school starts at 6:30 in the morning, when it is still dark in winter. And sometimes the Senate has evening sessions and it is dark

Here I am with Senator Javits of New York, discussing a proposed resolution.

when the pages go home. They said that this would be very dangerous for girls.

I then showed all the male pages a picture of Ellen McConnell, a very pretty nominee. I asked if any of them would volunteer to walk her over to the school

With Senator Dirksen—colleague and friend.

and to walk her home in the dark. When they saw the picture, all fourteen pages volunteered to walk with her —morning and night.

Then some senators said that pages had to carry some very heavy things, and girls were not strong enough.

I told them that I watched all of the pages for several weeks and had personally lifted some of their loads. I saw one of them carrying a package of Life Savers. Another brought a glass of water to a senator. I saw a page carrying three or four *Congressional Record*s, which were not that heavy. Besides, Ellen McConnell had been the winner of the President's Physical Fitness Award for two years in a row. She could handle anything that I saw the boy pages handle.

Then I was told that when the vote bell rings, the pages are sent all around to notify the senators that there is a vote coming up, and one of the stops was the men's washroom. You couldn't send a girl in there.

I pointed out the fact that Margaret Chase Smith, the former senator from Maine, had the best attendance record in the history of the Senate. And it wasn't because the boy pages had gone into the women's rest room to get her out and tell her that there was a vote coming up.

We actually had a public hearing on the subject. After the hearing, this foolish example of male chauvinism was wiped out. Girls were permitted to become pages, and ever since, they have been extraordinarily good pages. In fact, one of my girl appointees became a floor manager —a supervisor over other pages.

What happened to Ellen McConnell, our first female page? She has done very well. She graduated from the University of Illinois with a major in the field of communications. She has worked for a cable television station, assisting in the preparation of newscasts. Right now, her future is undecided. Not because she can't find a job, but because she can't decide whether to stay in communications, enter the political press area, or, believe it or not, get into the field of textiles. You see, she got hooked on textiles while she was working in a fabric store.

SOME
CONCERNS

I WOULD LIKE TO TELL you about a few of the things that most concern me. One of the big ones is the problem of secrecy in the whole governmental process. I believe very strongly in what we call "sunshine legislation." I say let the light come in. Let the people know what is going on.

Many senators agree with me that secrecy in government is one of the reasons why confidence in government has lessened in recent years. The people have found out about secret corruption and influence peddling that have been going on under the table, and they have begun to demand that everything be done out in the open in order to prevent dishonesty.

Then, too, people sometimes feel that it is hard to gain access to government leaders because too much goes on behind closed doors. Government often seems to be too remote and unconcerned with the problems of the people.

In a recent Louis Harris poll, people were asked if they felt that more problems could be solved if there were not so much secrecy in government. Seventy-one per cent thought that they could. They felt that secrecy in government was holding back our chances to move ahead as a nation.

There is rarely any reason for the Senate to shut the doors and keep the public out. We are doing business for all Americans, and the public has a right to see what is happening. Anyone should have the opportunity to see how we write bills and formulate legislation, because these things affect the entire American public. What do we have to hide?

Another concern is the proposed Twenty-sixth Amendment to the Constitution of the United States. That is the Equal Rights Amendment, and I was a cosponsor of it. It was designed to help give equal rights to women, and I believe that it is needed. In such areas as getting a job, getting a charge account from a store, getting equal pay, and getting equal opportunities for promotion, women have been discriminated against. We already have laws against discrimination because of race, religion, and age. Why not a law against discrimination because of sex?

I want women to have the same opportunities as men in anything that they might want to do in life. I want us to remove all forms of discrimination. I'm sure that we cannot legislate laws that will drive out all forms of prejudice. I know that an amendment to the Constitution will not make discrimination disappear. But it would be a start.

I am also concerned with sex discrimination that may not be so apparent. For instance, what do you

Women and men should be equal.

think of a statement like this? "Little girls should become nurses. Little boys should become doctors. Little girls should become secretaries. Little boys should become executives. Little girls need lawyers. But little boys should become lawyers."

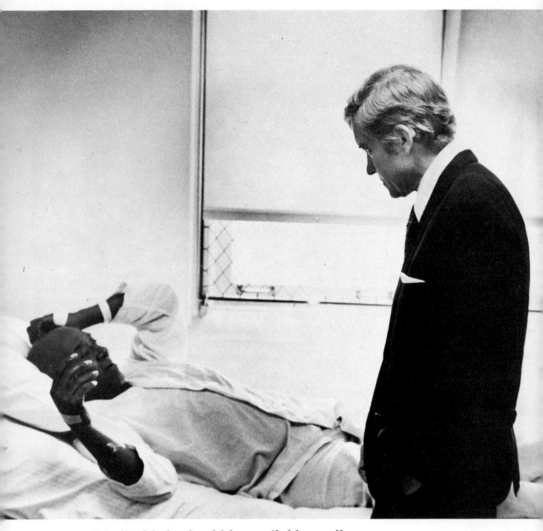

Medical help should be available to all.

That's terrible. But a statement like that was found in an elementary school textbook that was partly paid for with federal funds. I don't think we should take tax money to pay for books that would teach children that kind of discrimination.

The elderly should have equal rights.

Why shouldn't a girl be a doctor if she wants, rather than a nurse? Why shouldn't a boy want to be a nurse rather than a doctor? Men do nursing in the Armed Forces, so what is wrong with them nursing in a civilian hospital? Why should only women be airline stewardesses, while only men are pilots? Is it the money? Pilots are paid three or four times what stewardesses are paid. I believe in equal opportunities for women.

Public health is another concern of mine. I was recently involved with a bill that would improve health insurance payments for the American people. It provided for the financing of health insurance in this way: The employer would pay 75 per cent of the premiums, and the employee would pay 25 per cent.

As it stands now, imperfect though the plan may be, poor people can usually get medical assistance. Rich people can pay for their own medical costs. But this bill was designed to help the working, middle-income citizen.

If middle-income persons have expensive illnesses, it is not long before they can be wiped out financially. They are not able to take care of their health needs if there is an illness in the family that lasts over a period of time.

Then there is the question of taxes—a question that is always with us. There is a great deal of unfairness in our tax laws, I know. Perhaps the group that suffers most is the very poor. I can't believe it makes sense for very poor people to pay federal income taxes at all. Congress is working to change the tax laws so that people who are at or below the poverty level will not have to pay federal taxes.

In a way, social security is also a tax. And we

should change the social security law to protect the "working poor." These are the people who have jobs but still do not make enough money to get along. Everyone who works has to pay social security taxes. But the poor are hardest hit by the amounts that are taken out of their pay. Somehow we must make this deduction fairer to the poor.

I have mentioned that I am very involved with foreign policy. Some people ask me why we should have to worry about what is happening in the other countries of the world. They say that we can get along all right by ourselves. But I don't agree.

This is too small a world. We are one world and one people now. I can say something on television here, Telstar can pick it up, broadcast it, and it can be heard halfway around the world in a fraction of a second. We have to think in terms of improving relations among people—no matter where they live.

We are very much affected by what goes on abroad. What if a foreign power dropped a missile or a hydrogen bomb on us? Would that affect us? Of course. So it is part of our duty to prevent them, if possible, from ever getting into a position where they can attack us successfully.

Doesn't it make sense for us to try to prevent another war by improving our foreign relations? What about the effects of Vietnam? Young men were drafted and taken away from their wives, families, and friends. Fifty thousand of them were killed. Hundreds of thousands were injured.

You can't measure the costs of those deaths and injuries. But in actual expense, the war cost us $140 bil-

What a senator says can be broadcast all over the world in a fraction of a second.

Senators must be concerned with what is going on all over the world. Here I am with Secretary of State Henry Kissinger, who can be an excellent source of information.

lion. That's $700 for every man, woman, and child in this country. Everyone paid for that war. Let's try to prevent another one.

Like almost everyone else in this country, I am concerned about inflation, recession, and unemployment. All three of these things are interlocked, but let's begin with the rise in prices. Let's take the automobile as an example. They cost more now than they used to, as everybody knows.

You pay more for a car now because the costs of manufacturing the cars have gone up. Raw materials are higher, and so are labor costs. But there are other reasons for price increases. Some of these reasons are certain laws that have been passed.

We now require by law that every car have seat belts and pollution control. Autos never used to have these things. We have required new flashing lights and bumpers that are much stronger. All of this costs extra money. In the meantime, the costs of materials go up, and more of the materials are necessary to build the car.

Then another thing can happen. The price of the car has gone up, which makes the taxes on it go up, too. This increases the cost of the car still more. So a lot of people may decide they can't afford a new car just yet. They hang on to their old automobiles. More and more cars pile up in the showrooms, and the car makers begin to make fewer and fewer cars. You don't make cars if you can't sell them.

The next step is that the auto workers start being laid off. They aren't needed in the factories if few cars are being manufactured. So we have unemployment during the time of inflation, and that leads to a recession.

64

The Senate is concerned, as everyone is, with unemployment. We senators feel that the federal government has an obligation toward the person who cannot find a job. One of the plans that we sponsored was to provide 75 per cent of the salary to any state, city, or local government that could not otherwise afford to fill a necessary public service position, such as librarian or hospital attendant.

This may not seem like much, but it is a great improvement. When my father was thrown out of a job during the Great Depression of the 1930s, there was no unemployment compensation, no social security, no nothing. The local government just delivered small baskets of food to our front door. We got awfully tired of Spanish rice. That was not only crude, but we thought that it was a bit cruel, too.

Today, when a person loses a job, he or she is usually eligible for unemployment insurance. This provides a bit of money to live on until he or she gets another job. It isn't much, but it is better than what was done forty years ago. But we still haven't eliminated unemployment.

So these have been my main present concerns. A lot of work needs to be done on them, but we are, slowly but surely, chipping away at the problems.

One of my favorite people—former Senator Sam Ervin of North Carolina.

SOME FOND MEMORIES

MANY OF THE MOST pleasant memories I have had in public life involve the significant people with whom I have come in contact—especially those people for whom I have had a great deal of respect. Some of the most memorable occasions have been when I discovered that, though I sometimes disagreed with a person's political views, I could still feel that he or she was someone to be admired. I have already mentioned my feelings about such people as President Eisenhower, Senator Dirksen, and Senator Douglas. But here are a few more.

I remember one of the greatest statesmen ever produced by the state of Illinois—Adlai E. Stevenson II, the father of our present junior senator. He had been governor of the state, ran but was defeated twice for the presidency, and ended up as our ambassador to the United Nations.

One of my memories about him has to do with a trip that I made to India. I was in Benares and was being shown around by a very fine street guide. He asked me who I was and where I came from. When I told him, he asked me, "Do you know my friend, Adlai Stevenson?"

I admitted that I did, and when I got back to the United States I wrote Mr. Stevenson a letter telling him about the incident. I also said to him that I was much impressed with his political abilities, since he had apparently organized such a great staff that he had a precinct captain in Benares, India.

He wrote back to me. He said he was very pleased that I had gotten to India because he felt that even Republicans should travel to find out what was going on in the world. Then he added, "But don't work my side of the street any more."

I first met Jerry Ford in Peoria, Illinois, in 1949 when we were both elected as two of the Ten Outstanding Young Men of the year by the United States Junior Chamber of Commerce. He has proved the wisdom of their choice since then. His 1976 campaign theme of candor, honesty, and openness is exactly the theme that I think deserves a high priority.

We have skied together at Boyne Mountain, Michigan. I had relatives in Grand Rapids, Michigan, his home town, and visited them during the summer for many years in a row.

We both look upon a swimming pool, lake, ocean, or river as the best possible place for exercise. And both of us would like to swim every day of our lives. The exception was when Jerry had to leave his home, which had

President Ford and I have been friends for years.

a pool, and move to the White House, where President Nixon had removed the pool. He was stuck for a while until the new White House pool was finished. During that time, I told him, as I swam in my own small pool in Georgetown, I had one thought. I'd say to myself, "Now, if I lived at 1600 Pennsylvania Avenue, I wouldn't be able to do this."

There is a strange thing about politics. Politicians of different parties sometimes get along better with each other than politicians of the same party. For instance, it is no secret that Governor Walker of Illinois and Mayor Richard Daley of Chicago—both Democrats—do not get along very well.

But I've always had a cordial relationship with Mayor Daley. One of the great days that I have spent with him was when the first astronauts to land on the moon came to Chicago for a triumphal celebration. I had served on the United States Senate Space Committee and had been closely acquainted with many of the details of our space program. I had worked closely with Dr. Wernher von Braun, a former leader of the National Aeronautics and Space Administration (NASA).

Mayor Daley invited me to participate in the celebration. I rode with him and the astronauts through the streets of Chicago and finally down State Street, the main street of Chicago's Loop. All of Chicago seemed to have turned out for the astronauts. By the time we reached the Michigan Avenue Bridge over the Chicago River and all of the fireboats were shooting jets of water into the air, I concluded that this was the finest celebration ever to occur in Chicago.

Richard Daley had participated, in his many years as mayor, in countless celebrations. But he said to me, "There was never one quite like this and probably never will be again."

Winston Churchill was the most impressive foreign politician that I ever met. I never knew him during his term in office, but I met him later in Washington when he came over to visit President Eisenhower.

However, one time, toward the end of his life, I found myself seated next to him on a plane flying from London to the south of France. I told him that years before, a London collector of rare books had put together a complete set of all of the writings of Winston Churchill, from his earliest to his latest, and had bound them in red leather, and that I had bought the complete set.

They were my most treasured possessions. As a public official, they had inspired me. But I had to admit to him that the stories of his early difficulties in school had been the source of the biggest satisfaction to my son, Roger, who early in life was not a particularly good student either.

I recalled that he had told of doing so poorly in school that he was not permitted to go on in Greek. He was required, instead, to continue his courses in English. I mentioned that he had concluded his autobiography with the words "Thank God I was forced to learn how to speak and write the English language." And I told him that many of the rest of us were also appreciative of this.

A smile settled over his face as he seemed to reflect upon his love of the English language and what he had done with it over the years to advance his own political cause and to save his beloved England.

IN THE
FUTURE

FIRST, MY FUTURE. People have often asked me if I would want to become President of the United States. Frankly, the answer is yes. But I don't see any openings. I have told President Ford that I intend to support him in 1976. I think that he is a man of decency, integrity, candor, and openness. He and the members of his administration know the job of the office of the President, and I feel that I can be most effective by staying in the Senate. As far as 1980 or 1984 goes, we'll just have to see.

Besides, the office of the President is overwhelming and the job is awesome. I think that whenever a person comes in contact with a President, he or she feels a certain awe and respect for the office, even though he or she may have known the man who occupies the office for a long time. I know that I feel this way.

I have known all of the recent Presidents, beginning with Harry Truman. And always, when I have walked into the Oval Office of the White House, I feel something special.

I have thought about the Presidency long enough to have some definite advice for those who want to run for this office, however. They must first be convinced that they are presidential material. This means that they have to keep reviewing their chances and conferring with advisers and friends. They must be sure that their decision would be acceptable to their families, because the family is always very much involved. And, of course, they must also feel there is a reasonable chance of being nominated by their party. Very few people have ever been successful in changing parties and becoming nominated for President by their new party. Wendell Willkie in the 1940s was successful, but John Lindsay, in the 1970s, was not.

Care must be taken in the selection of the vice-presidential candidate. I believe that this person needs only one major qualification. The vice-presidential nominee should be the person who would make the best President if the Chief Executive could not serve a full term.

That's all that I think a Vice-president needs going for him. Many people think that the ticket should include a religious balance. If, for example, the presidential candidate is a Protestant, the vice-presidential candidate should be a Catholic.

Others believe in a geographical balance. If one

Families can help a lot on the campaign trail. Here my wife and I are starting a tour of the state of Illinois.
(METRO NEWS PHOTOS)

member of the ticket is from the Midwest, the other should be from the East or South or West.

I think that these considerations are relatively unimportant compared to the consideration of who is the best person to take the President's place.

I have often thought of what I might be doing if I were not a senator. I might well be still in business, or I might be teaching. I might even be the president of a college, as my son-in-law, Jay, was.

He had experienced an election defeat, as I once did. When he was defeated for the governorship of the state of West Virginia, he accepted the job as president of West Virginia Wesleyan College. I called him up the next morning and said, "Good morning, Mr. President."

He answered me, "Say that again. It sounds good."

If I ever did leave politics, I think that I would like to go into some sort of philanthropic work—something like working for an educational foundation. Then, too, I love to teach, and I learn a great deal by being with young people who ask good questions and have inquisitive minds.

But I have never really thought about getting out of politics. At least, not at this stage. I've really been in it as an elected official for a little over ten years. And I was in business for twenty-five years. I am in my midfifties, and I certainly hope that I can stay active in politics for many more years.

We are nearing the end of the book, and I can't bring myself to finish it without trying to give some advice to you young readers. Try to be successful in any career you undertake. Take advantage of every day of

I love to teach.

your lives. When each day ends, you will never have it to live over again.

Learn as much as you can in school. Learn as much as you can in your neighborhood. And keep adding to your knowledge. Discipline yourselves to have good study habits and good work habits. Some people never learn how to study well or work well, you know.

Some people never learn to define their problems. You must learn how to define and solve your problems wisely. The principles of solving problems are the same whether you are in the Senate, running a small business, or studying in school. Learn where to go to find information that will help you to solve the problem.

Every day, solve the problems that confront you. Learn to get along better with others. All these things will help you in the future.

Finally, let me get in a plug for choosing a political career. You can start right now, and it will be a rewarding experience. Learn how the political process works by engaging in someone else's campaign. Eventually you may be running a campaign of your own.

And learn something of the law. It is probably one of the most wonderful ideas that man has ever invented.

CHARLES H. PERCY was born in Pensacola, Florida, and received his A.B. from the University of Chicago in 1941. Before running for the Senate in 1966, he had been the president and then chairman of the board of Bell & Howell. He is now the senior senator from the state of Illinois and divides his time between his home in Wilmette, Illinois, and his offices in Chicago and Washington, D.C.

INDEX

Adams, John, 47
Aged, the. *See* Elderly, the
Alaska: representatives from, 34; senators from, 34
Ambassadors, as part of the executive branch of government, 33
Arab countries, Senator Percy's visit to, 12
Arizona, senators from, 35–36
Astronauts, 70
Automobiles (auto workers), 64; inflation and recession and, 64

Bartlett, Dewey F., 14
Bell & Howell Company, 21, 22, 26–28; Senator Percy as president and chairman of the board of, 21, 22, 26–28

Benares, India, Senator Percy in, 68
Bicentennial (1976), 24
Bills, legislative, introduction, "marking up," and passage of, 41–48
Boyne Mountain, Mich., 68
Buchwald, Art, 14

Cabinet members, as part of the executive branch of government, 33
Calhoun, John C., 37
California, 15; representatives from, 34; senators from, 34
Cambodia, 47
Chicago, Ill., 9, 12, 21, 34, 70; celebration for astronauts in, 70; gun control legislation and, 45–46

Chicago, University of, 12, 21, 28, 79

Chiefs of Staff, Joint, 33

Children (*see also* Girls; Students; Young people) : and education, 58, 77–78; and sex discrimination and equal opportunity legislation, 57–60

Churchill, Winston S., 70–71

Citizens (*see also* Working people) : and right to suggest legislation, 40–41

Commission on National Goals, 24–25

Committee meetings, United States Senate, 3, 4

Congress (congressmen and congresswomen), 34 (*see also* House of Representatives; Senate, United States) ; and declaration of war, 47–48; as the legislative branch of government, 34; and making laws, 39–48; number of members of, 34; and the President and separation of powers, 47–48; and recesses, 9–12

Congressional districts, 34

Congressional Record, The, 1, 52

Constitution, United States, 37, 45, 47; and declaration of war, 47–48; Founding Fathers and, 33, 47; and separation of powers, 33, 47; Twenty-sixth (Equal Rights) Amendment, 56–60

Constitutional Convention, 47

Corruption in government, 55

Courts, federal, 33

Daley, Richard J., 70

"Decisions for a Better America" (Republican Committee on Program and Progress report), 25

Democratic party (Democrats), 22, 24, 46, 70; and Senate pages, 48; senators, 36, 39; and whip in Senate, 39

Dirksen, Everett M., 29, 31, 49, 51, 67

Discrimination (*see also* Sex discrimination) : Twenty-sixth Amendment and, 56–60

Dishonesty in government, 55

Douglas, Paul H., 28–30, 67; described, 28–30

Economy (economic issues), legislation and, 60–61, 64–65

Education: importance for young people of, 77–78; sex discrimination and, 58–60

Eisenhower (Dwight D.) Administration, 24–25, 26, 67, 71; described, 25; State of the Union message (1959), 24–25; and support for Senator Percy, 25, 26

Eisenhower, Milton, 25

Elderly, the, equal rights for, 56, 59

Employment (and unemployment), federal government and legislation and, 64–65

Equal opportunity laws, 46,

56–60; Twenty-sixth
Amendment, 56–60
Equal Rights (Twenty-sixth)
Amendment, 56–60
Ervin, Sam J., Jr., 66
Executive branch of government,
33

Fannin, Paul, as the senior
senator from Arizona, 36
Farmers, in the United States
Senate, 36
Federal government. *See*
Government, United States
Federal income taxes, 60
Ford (Gerald R.)
Administration, 38, 39, 68–70,
73; described, 68, 70
Ford Foundation, Fund for Adult
Education of, 12
Foreign policy (foreign
relations), 61–64
Foreign Relations Committee,
Senate, 5
Founding Fathers, 33, 47
Fund for Adult Education of the
Ford Foundation, 12

Girls (*see also* Children;
Students; Women; Young
people) : as Senate pages,
49–53
Goldwater, Barry, as the junior
senator from Arizona, 35–36
Government, United States (*see
also* Congress; House of
Representatives; Senate,
United States) : corruption and

secrecy in, 55–56; and economy
(economic issues), 60–61,
64–65; and legislation (*see*
Laws) ; separation of powers
and three coequal branches of,
33–34 (*see also* individual
branches, *e.g.*, Executive
branch of government) ; and
taxes, 60–61, 64; and war and
foreign policy and relations,
61–64
Grand Rapids, Mich., 68
Great Depression (1930s), 65
Green, Rita, 14
Gun control legislation, 39–41,
45–46

Hamilton, Alexander, 47
Handguns. *See* Gun control
legislation
Harris (Louis) poll, on secrecy in
government, 56
Health insurance, 60
House of Representatives, 1, 34
(*see also* Congress) ; as the
legislative branch of
government, 34; and making of
laws, 43–48; terms of office in,
34
Hughes, Ed, 14
Humphrey, Hubert H., 31
Hydrogen bomb, 61

Illinois, 9, 12 (*see also* Chicago,
Ill.; Peoria, Ill.; Springfield,
Ill.) ; 1964 elections, 28; 1966
elections, 28–30; 1972
elections, 30; pages in United

States Senate from, 49;
representatives in Congress
from, 34; senior and junior
senators from, 35
Illinois, University of, 52
Income taxes, federal, 60
India, Senator Percy's visit to, 68
Indian Embassy (Washington,
D.C.), 5–8
Inflation, economic, 64–65
Influence peddling, 55
Insurance: health, 60;
unemployment, 65
Iran, Senator Percy's visit to, 12
Israel, Senator Percy's visit to, 12

Javits, Jacob K., 48, 49, 50; and
girls as pages in the United
States Senate, 49
Jefferson, Thomas, 36, 47
Jobs, federal government and.
See Employment (and
unemployment)
Johns Hopkins University, 25
Johnson (Lyndon B.)
Administration, 14, 39
Joint Chiefs of Staff, 33
Judicial branch of government,
33
Junior Chamber of Commerce,
United States, 68
Junior and senior senators, 34–36

Kennedy, John F. (Jack), 14
Kennedy Center for the
Performing Arts, Senator Percy
on the board of, 12
Kentucky, 8–9

Kissinger, Henry A., 63
Korea, 47
Kothe, Alison, 14

Laos, 47
Laws (legislation) : citizens and
the right to suggest, 40; debate
and, 46–47; discrimination and
equal rights and, 46, 56–60;
economy (economic issues)
and, 64, 65; introduction,
"marking up," and passage of
bills into, 41–48; making of,
39–48; and public health, 60;
road blocks and red tape and,
46–48; secrecy and, 55, 56;
Senate and, 39–48; social
security and, 60–61; taxes and,
60–61
Lawyers, in the United States
Senate, 36
Legislation. *See* Laws
(legislation)
Legislative branch of government,
34. *See also* Congress; House of
Representatives; Senate,
United States
Legislative Reference Bureau,
Library of Congress, 41
Library of Congress, Legislative
Reference Bureau of, 41
Lindsay, John V., 74
Los Angeles, Calif., congressional
districts in, 34

McConnell, Ellen, as the first
female page in United States
Senate, 50–53

Maddox, Donna, 14
Madison, James, 36, 47
Mansfield, Mike, 31
"Marking up the bill," 41–43
Medical help legislation, 58, 60
Middle East, Senator Percy's visit
  to, 12
"Morning hour," Senate's, 4

National Aeronautics and Space
  Administration (NASA), 70
New York, N.Y., congressional
  districts in, 34
Nielson, Art, 22
Nielsen (A. C.) Company, 22
Nixon (Richard M.)
  Administration, 39, 69
North Korea, 47
North Vietnam, 47

Pages, United States Senate, 5,
  48–53; girls as, 49–53;
  qualifications for and
  appointment of, 48; what they
  do, 48
Parliamentarian, United States
  Senate, 41
Peoria, Ill., 68
Percy, Charles H., 1–19; activities
  as a United States Senator,
  1–19, 39–53; advice to young
  people given by, 76–78; and
  baseball, 12–14; as a
  businessman, 21, 22, 26–28; as
  chairman of the 1960 Platform
  Committee of the Republican
  National Convention, 25–26;
  as chairman of the Republican
Committee on Program and
  Progress, 25–26; and Christmas
  parties for his staff, 14; and the
  Commission on National Goals,
  24, 25; and congressional
  recesses, 9–12; and "Decisions
  for a Better America" report,
  25; on discrimination and
  equal rights and legislation,
  56–60; on economy (economic
  issues), 60–61, 64–65; and
  education, 79 (see also
  Education); elected as one of
  the Ten Outstanding Young
  Men (1949), 68; elected to the
  United States Senate from
  Illinois, 28–30; at embassy and
  dinner receptions, 5–8; and
  family, 15–19; and fond
  memories of people, 67–71; on
  foreign policy and relations,
  61–64; future plans of, 73–76;
  and girls as pages in the United
  States Senate, 48–53; and
  grandchildren, 15–19; interest
  in law, 21; interest in work of
  foundations and educational
  institutions, 12; and legislative
  sessions and programs, 4, 5,
  39–53; and letter-writing
  (mail), 2, 12; and loss of race
  for governor of Illinois (1964),
  28, 31–32; and meetings with
  people (voters), 4–5, 9, 12;
  and official trips abroad, 12,
  68; and philanthropic work,
  76; and political affiliation as
  a Republican, 22; on political
  careers for young people, 78; as
  president and chairman of the

board of Bell & Howell Company, 21, 22, 26–28; and "Prospects for America" report, 22; and reading, 1; and recreation and sports, 12–15, 68–70; re-elected to the United States Senate for a second six-year term, 30, 32; and Senate committee meetings, 3, 4; and skiing, 15, 24, 68; and specific individuals (*see* specific individuals by name); and speeches, 8–9; and staff, size and description of, 12, 14; and staff meetings, 3–4, 5; and start of political career, 21–32; and students in politics, 30, 31–32, 78; swearing in as a United States Senator, 31; and swimming, 15, 68–70; and teaching, 76, 77; and telephone calls, 2, 5, 7, 12; and tennis, 1, 14–15; as a trustee of the University of Chicago, 12; and weekend activities, 9–12; and working lunches as a senator, 4; and World War II service, 21

Percy, Mrs. Charles H., 5, 75
Percy, Roger, 71
Permanent Investigations Subcommittee, Senate, 3
Political careers, young people and choice of, 78
Pollution control, legislation and, 64
Poor people: medical assistance and insurance and, 60; social security and, 60–61; taxes and, 60–61

Prejudice. *See* Discrimination
President (presidency), United States, 33, 73–74, 76 (*see also* specific individuals and administrations by name); as Commander in Chief of the Armed Forces, 48; and Congress and separation of powers, 47–48; and declaration of war power, 47–48; and Senate, 39; and separation of powers principle, 47–48; and signing of bills into law, 45; and vetoes, 45
President's Physical Fitness Award, 52
Prices, rising (inflation), 64
Problems, young people and defining and solving of, 77–78
"Prospects for America" (Rockefeller Brothers Studies Project report), 22
Public health, legislation, and, 58, 60
Public television, 12

Recesses, congressional, 9–12
Recession, economic, 64–65
Relief funds, bills to provide, 47
Representatives, 34. *See also* House of Representatives
Republican Committee on Program and Progress, 25–26
Republican National Committee, 22
Republican National Convention, 1960 Platform Committee of, 25–26

Republican party (Republicans),
22, 24, 25–26, 28, 29, 46;
senators, 36, 39; and Senate
pages, 48, 49; whip in Senate,
39
Ribicoff, Abraham A., 3
Rockefeller, Jay, 22, 23, 76
Rockefeller Brothers Studies
Project, 22
Rothemal, Bud, 22

Saturday night specials
(handguns), legislation to
control, 39–41, 45–46
Seat belts, legislation and, 64
Seattle, Wash., 15
Secrecy in government, 55–56
Senate, United States, 1, 33–53
(see also Senators, United
States) ; committee meetings, 3,
4; congressional recesses, 9–12;
leadership in, 39; as the
legislative branch of
government, 34; and legislative
programs and sessions, 4, 5,
39–53; make-up of, 36–37; and
making of laws, 39–48;
"morning hour," 4; pages in,
48–53; parliamentarian in, 41;
party whips and leadership in,
39; presiding officer of, 37–39;
and secrecy, 56; Vice-president
as presiding officer of, 37, 39;
voting in, 39, 43; working
lunches in, 4
Senate Foreign Relations
Committee, 5
Senate Space Committee, 70
Senators, United States (see also

Senate, United States; specific
individuals by name) : and law
degrees, 36; minimum age for,
36; number of, 34; senior and
junior, 34–36; term of office of,
34; varied backgrounds of,
36–37
Senior and junior senators, 34–36
Separation of powers, branches of
government and, 33, 47–48;
and declaration of war, 47–48;
Founding Fathers and idea of,
33
Sex discrimination: Equal Rights
(Twenty-sixth) Amendment
and, 56–60; female Senate
pages and, 49–53
Smith, Margaret Chase, 36, 52
Social security, 60–61, 65
Space program, 70
Speeches (speechmaking),
Senator Percy and, 8–9
Springfield, Ill., 9, 12, 35
Stennis, John C., 48
Stevenson, Adlai E., II, 67–68;
described, 67–68
Stevenson, Adlai E., III, 13, 14,
35, 67; as the junior senator
from Illinois, 35
Students (see also Education;
Young people) : and politics,
30, 31–32, 78
Study habits, importance to
young people of self-discipline
and, 77
Subcommittees, congressional,
legislation and, 41–43
"Sunshine legislation," secrecy in
government and, 55
Sun Valley, Idaho, 24

Supreme Court, United States, 33, 45

Taft, Robert A., 5
Taxes, 58, 60–61, 64
Television: public, 12; Telstar, 61; "Today" program, 1
Telstar, 61
Ten Outstanding Young Men of the Year award, United States Junior Chamber of Commerce, 68
"Today" (television program), 1
Truman, Harry S, 74
Twenty-sixth (Equal Rights) Amendment, 56–60

Unemployment. See Employment (and unemployment)
United States Government. See Government, United States
United States Junior Chamber of Commerce, 68

Van Buren, Martin, 37
Veterans for the Republican Party, 22
Vetoes, presidential, 45; overriding of, 45
Vice-president (vice-presidency), office of, 33, 74–76; care needed in selection of, 74–76; and geographical balance in selection of, 74–76; as presiding officer of the Senate, 37, 39; and religion in selection of, 74
Vietnam War, 47, 61
Von Braun, Dr. Wernher, 70

Walker, Daniel T., 15, 35, 70
War: foreign policy and relations and cost of, 61–62; separation of powers and declaration of, 47
Ward, Greg, 14
Weapons control. See Gun control legislation
Weicker, Lowell, 14
West Virginia, 15
West Virginia Wesleyan College, 76
Whips, party, Senate leadership and, 39
Willkie, Wendell L., 74
Wilmette, Ill., 79
Women: discrimination and equal rights for, 56–60; as Senate pages, 49–53; as senators, 36
Work habits, importance to young people of self-discipline and, 77
Working people (middle-income people): and inflation, recession and unemployment, 64–65; and medical assistance, 60; and taxes, 60, 61
World War II, 21, 47

Young people (see also Children; Girls; Students): advice by Senator Percy to, 76–78; and choosing political careers, 78; and learning about the law, 78; and problem-solving, 77–78; as Senate pages, 48–53; and study and work habits, 77; and success in careers, 76–78